FAIRIES

THE COTTINGLEY PHOTOGRAPHS
AND THEIR SEQUEL

Photograph Number One:

FRANCES AND THE FAIRIES

Photograph taken in July 1917 by Elsie. Camera, Midg Quarter. Distance about, 4 feet. Time, 1/50th second. Sunny day.

The original negative is asserted by expert photographers to bear not the slightest trace of combination work, re-touching, or anything whatever to mark it as other than a straight single-exposure photograph taken in the open air under natural conditions. The negative was a little over-exposed. The waterfall and rocks are about 20 feet distance behind Frances, who is standing in shallow water inside the bank of the beck. The colouring of the fairies was described by the girls as shades of green, lavender and mauve, most marked in the wings and fading to almost pure white in the limbs and drapery.

FAIRIES

THE COTTINGLEY PHOTOGRAPHS
AND THEIR SEQUEL

By

EDWARD L. GARDNER

THE THEOSOPHICAL PUBLISHING HOUSE LTD.
68 GREAT RUSSELL STREET
LONDON, WC1B 3BU

ADYAR, INDIA   WHEATON, ILL.—USA

© 1966 Theosophical Publishing House Ltd.

First published . . . 1945
Second edition . . . 1951
Third edition 1957
Fourth and revised edition 1966
Reprinted 1972

ISBN 7229 5011 X

Printed in Great Britain by
Fletcher & Son Ltd, Norwich

PREFACE

As a preface to a book that submits some practical evidence of the existence of fairy creatures—and also of higher levels of this other order of being—the following extract from the late Cardinal Newman's *Apologia** is appropriate and significant:

'I suppose it was to the Alexandrian School and to the early Church that I owe in particular what I definitely held about the angels. I viewed them not only as the ministers employed by the Creator . . . but as carrying on the economy of the visible world. I considered them as the real causes of motion, light and life and of those elementary principles of the physical universe which, when offered in their developments to our senses, suggest to us the notion of cause and effect and of what are called the laws of nature. I have drawn out this doctrine in my sermon for Michaelmas day written not later than 1834. I say of the angels "Every breath of air and ray of light and heat, every beautiful prospect is, as it were, the skirts of their garments, the waving of the robes of those whose faces see God". Again, I ask, what would be the thoughts of a man who "when examining a flower or a herb or a pebble or a ray of light, which he treats as something so beneath him in the scale of existence, suddenly discovered that he was in the presence of some powerful being who was hidden behind the visible things he was inspecting, who, though concealing his wise hand, was giving them their beauty, grace and perfection, as being God's instruments for the purpose, nay, whose robe and ornaments those objects were which he was so eager to analyse?" '

* *Apologia Pro Vita Sua* by Cardinal Newman, Everyman Edition, page 50.

CONTENTS

ILLUSTRATIONS

INTRODUCTION TO THE 1966 EDITION

This book was first issued over twenty years ago. The material in it goes back to 1917 and first received publicity through Sir Arthur Conan Doyle's articles in the *Strand Magazine* in 1928. Since then a great deal of knowledge about the human mind has been added to what was known even in 1945, let alone earlier. The question then arose as to whether the text in so debatable a subject as fairies would be suitable today or whether it should be rewritten. On careful scrutiny, however, it was found that the first or factual part was admirably objective, and that the later parts, though they might be added to in terms of modern knowledge, were not such as lent themselves to drastic correction or contradiction. Moreover, to try to rewrite the book would change it and ruin it. So it was agreed to let the original text stand, and to put with it, as an introduction, material derived from modern work in depth psychology, parapsychology, and any other relevant field.

Parapsychology and depth psychology are doing much towards studying the structure of the human mind, but it would be no exaggeration to say that they have taken only a first short step towards opening up the subject. That that step is towards the ancient perennial doctrines about man and the world or worlds he lives in, and not away from it, is one of the things that surprises and disconcerts the materialist. Nevertheless it is so. And this book, in what it suggests, seems to lie in effect between the two points of view, being too indecisive for the scientist and too materialistic and matter of fact for the spiritual philosopher. Nevertheless it can be said to have its place in the whole, if only in the questions it raises.

Many people claim to have seen fairies, angels, and the like. They are often unsophisticated simple folk, but by no means always so. Cardinal Newman, quoted at the beginning of this book, evidently discovered for himself what theosophical students would call the Devic or Angelic kingdom, about which, though the word 'angel' constantly occurs in scripture and ritual, there is no proper eschatology in orthodox Christianity. There are many other responsible and balanced people who, in their own way, have had similar experience.

To many people there is little doubt as to the genuineness of the photographs in the book, but naturally there are others who tend to doubt them. If this is so, how do they explain them in general terms, and in this particular instance? Nobody has *scientifically* explained the mechanism by which what spiritualists call 'extras' are produced on a film, and still less the exact nature of what is actually represented. In a small number of instances the 'extra' is clear enough to be recognized as, say, the face of a particular individual; but in most cases the people are unknown. It does not follow from this that the soul of a dead person is involved. Our minds are full of images and memories of people and events that have come within the range of our senses, but to which we have paid no conscious attention. Such things nevertheless leave an impression on the unconscious mind, and it may well be that for some reason a particular trace is, as it were, picked out of the memory-file. Many people are aware that sometimes when half asleep a whole stream of clear images passes before their mental eyes, yet by no effort can any personal meaning or memory be linked with them. The unconscious registration of all kinds of things of no particular interest or moment to ourselves may account for this phenomenon and also for the 'extras' already mentioned.

This still does not tell us just how the link is made between the mind and the chemical matter of the film *except* that a medium is an essential element in the process. This applies equally to the photographs in George de la Warr's *Worlds Beyond the Atom*, all of which depended on the presence of a certain person at the time they were taken. As we learn more about 'psycho-kinesis' we may evolve a clearer pattern of this mechanism which, in theosophical terms, depends on the quality of the etheric or vital field, the *prana mayakosha* of the Hindus. This is, however, too big a subject for study here; it can be pursued elsewhere.

In this book we have a special case where, apparently, non-human and non-physical creatures were photographed. Adolescents, and perhaps especially girls, are often mediumistic, if only for a time, which would account for one aspect of the pictures. The medium was there.

The next question is what was being photographed? Clearly most of the fairies were lamentably conventional and sophisticated, even if they appear to be moving. The movement is easily accounted for, because a girl imagining a dancing fairy would quite naturally think of motion; her 'thought-form' would not be static. We know, moreover, that 'eidetic images'. are fairly common and easily produced. They are as it were 'thought-forms' detached in some measure from the control of the thinker, and they form the basis of the majority of visions of gods, angels, demons, saints, masters, and so on. It is therefore possible to account for these photographs solely in terms of self-projected imagination. But there are certain factors that perhaps do not altogether fit in with this.

Photograph V shows something apparently unknown to the girls, but reported by others who claim to have observed fairies. The cloudy ragged appearance of 'ectoplasm' is common in mediumistic circles where people 'sit for development', and in genuine spiritualistic photography.

So far there is therefore little mystery about the photographs. The next question is whether fairies, nature spirits, etc. really exist. Here we have the universal and age-old tradition about the existence of non-physical entities.

Kant suggests that such traditions cannot be summarily dismissed. Certain scientists, Sir Alister Hardy for instance, tend to think of a 'paraphysical' stream of life as lying behind evolutionary processes. They would certainly not think in terms of a fairy world, but they would express this more in terms of energies which guide evolution from within, just as external factors—environment, climate, and so on—do from outside. Therefore it would seem that in an environment well away from human habitation these 'foci of nature' would be vibrantly ready to draw around themselves, and thus animate, the 'thought-forms' of the two girls. Otherwise why did the girls not see the fairies in their own home or garden?

Are we here seeing the effects of a coincidence between these natural energies and the human ideational evolutionary forces given form by the children's own minds, these being reinforced by age-long tradition about fairies, gnomes, elementals and other creatures associated with Nature? Such a possibility cannot be ruled out. It would be interesting to know whether, had the girls been, let us say, Indian, Chinese, or Negro, the images would have been other than so blatantly Northern European in appearance. It seems likely that this would be so, even if the Indian, Chinese, or Negro were taking photographs in an English dell, but of this we cannot be sure. What is certain is the ability of the mind to project images which originate entirely from within itself.

Apart from the factual material, we now need to look at some of the theoretical considerations. On page 32 Mr. Gardner explains that mediumship and clairvoyance are two separate things, though—as in this case—they can occur in the same person. He adds also that it seems as if both girls needed to be present to get good photographs. This is in line with other mediumistic phenomena where several people have to join in a circle to strengthen the medium's own powers.

The 'etheric eyes' of which he speaks are, of course, unknown to science, but it is established that the range of perceptivity of physical organs sometimes extends beyond their legitimate limits, becoming what is called extra-sensory. Further extension, however, let us say, of visual extra-sensory impressions would have to come, not through the etheric eye, but through the centre physically situated in the forehead above the nose, known in the East as the *Ajna chakram*.

For the rest, and particularly the reports of other clairvoyants, it is most important that the reader should realize how strong is the personal element in any description. This is true of any and every clairvoyant, no matter who he may be. What is reported must never be taken as factual in any absolute sense. It is the investigator's view of certain facts seen through his own mental preconceptions. Thus many people describe angels or devas as quasi-human in appearance, and often draw pictures of them as glorified human beings surrounded by patterns of ethereal but coloured streams of energy. Others—

seemingly more objective—do not see any kind of human form, but observe moving patterns of fine energies which flow in and out, producing exquisite effects, which are never static. Others believe these observations to be purely the product of the observer's mind. At the same time one may well ask oneself whether what we know as the human form may not be a basic archetype throughout certain realms of nature, so that fairies, angels, etc. have a form akin to ours. All vertebrate animals have, like us, eyes, nose, mouth, limbs in broadly the same pattern. Why not certain classes of non-physical entities? This is a question that must be left open.

In short, while this book is already highly suggestive, it raises a number of cogent points. Some of these must remain unanswerable in our present state of knowledge; others are at least partly explicable, and yet others can be amplified by a study of traditional scriptural literature, and also from other books by theosophical students.

Whatever one may conclude about the validity of the photographs, one thing is beyond doubt: the complete integrity and objectivity of the author.

Phoebe D. Bendit

PART I

THE COTTINGLEY FAIRY PHOTOGRAPHS

Fairy Photographs Published

The Christmas number of the *Strand Magazine* in the year 1920 contained an article by Sir Arthur Conan Doyle and myself, entitled 'An Epoch-making Event—Fairies Photographed.' The magazine was on the bookstalls at the beginning of December, and the issue was sold out in three days. Very much public interest was aroused; in fact, the magazine story spread around the world, and many newspapers referred to the photographs and narrative, naturally with reserve and, in some cases, with frank criticism. Both the photographic and personal evidence submitted at the time were shortly afterwards tested and probed to the limits possible by photographers, news-reporters and many private investigators.

A year or so later Sir Arthur wrote a book on the subject under the title of *The Coming of the Fairies*, published by Hodder & Stoughton, and a second edition of this appeared a few years after that, about 1928 (long since sold out). Many years have passed since the first publication was issued, and in no particular, then or since, has any flaw been discovered in the evidence presented, nor any trace of deceit or fraud. Indeed, further corroboration has presented itself from an unexpected source.

'An Epoch-making Event'? Yes, if true. So, in response to many requests, I have set down here in careful sequence a plain and straightforward account of the way our investigation opened and of the course we took to disprove or establish the genuineness of the photographs. The subject and the incidents are well worth such a record at first-hand. Most people know something today of the possibilities of faked photography, and the reader can form his own opinion as to whether we were justified in reaching the conclusions we did.

The First Photographs

It was a morning in May 1920 that the post brought me two small prints, with a covering letter from a friend asking for my opinion. One print showed a group of fairy-like figures dancing on the bank of a stream in front of a little girl, and on the other was a winged gnome-like creature near a girl's beckoning hand. The letter merely stated that they were taken some time since by two girls in Yorkshire. My friend, it seemed, had mentioned 'fairies' in a lecture, and a woman had approached afterwards to ask if the lecturer thought that 'fairies were really true?' If so, said the woman, then two photographs which her young daughter had taken 'might be true after all'—though, she added, neither she nor her husband

Photograph Number Two:

ELSIE AND THE GNOME

Photograph taken in September 1917 by Frances. Camera, the Midg.

The original negative has been tested, enlarged and analysed in the same exhaustive manner as the first, and declared to be a perfectly straight single-exposure photograph, rather badly under-exposed. The site is at the top of the bank of the glen and is a stretch of level grass bounded by a stone wall on the left. Elsie was playing with the gnome and beckoning it to come on to her knee. The gnome leapt up just as Frances, who had the camera, snapped the shutter. He is described as wearing black tights, a reddish jersey and a pointed bright red cap. Elsie said there was no perceptible weight, though when on the bare hand the feeling is like a 'little breath'. The wings were more moth-like than the fairies and of a soft neutral tint. Elsie explained that what seem to be markings on his wings are simply his pipes, which he was swinging in his grotesque little left hand. The music of the pipes can only just be heard as a tiny little tinkle if everything is quite still. Neither of the children could distinguish any tune.

had been able to believe it. The next day the prints were brought to my friend and then were forwarded to me, as I was known to be interested in examples of abnormal photography.

The two prints (see Photographs Numbers 1 and 2, frontispiece and facing page 16) did not appeal to me at first at all seriously. They looked uncommonly like an ordinary studio fake, or merely photographs of a picture, or a doctored plate such as had been plentifully produced in the name of spirit-photography, and with which I was more than familiar. So I just wrote to say that a print was of little use for testing purposes, and could the negatives be sent. I quite expected to hear no more. A few days later, however, a small cardboard box came enclosing two quarter-plate negatives on glass and a note from a Mrs. Wright, of Cottingley, near Bradford, to say that her daughter Elsie had taken them in a glen near the cottage where they lived; nothing more. The negative of the group certainly looked better, for it bore no trace of double-exposure that I could detect; it was, in fact, a very good clear snapshot. The second one of the single figure was badly under-exposed, little detail could be made out, and the girl's hand was abnormal. The very poorness of its quality, though, was a point perhaps in its favour. Anyway, I thought them at least worth an expert's careful examination, and I determined to get this before replying. I knew a Mr. Snelling slightly, a photographer who had recently set up in business of his own, and at once I made an enquiry of the firm for whom he had worked for a long time as to his qualifications. The reply was encouraging and amusing, for it seemed that studio work had been his speciality for many years. The manager said in conclusion: 'What Snelling doesn't know about faked photography isn't worth knowing.' This was the very kind of expert I wanted.

To Harrow, then, I took the two quarter-plates, saw Mr. Snelling and, without preliminaries, asked him to make a few prints of both, with a hope that he could strengthen the under-exposed plate. He took the negatives, smiled a little as he glanced at them, and started to ask a question, but stopped. 'Wait a moment,' he said, and went over to a glass-topped desk, switched on a light underneath, placed the first negative on the top and began examining it with sundry lenses. He spent so long over it that I broke in with the question as to what interested him. The reply was something of a shock. 'Several things,' said Snelling. 'This plate is a single-exposure; these dancing figures are not made of paper nor of any fabric; they are not painted on a photographed background—but what gets me most is that all these figures have *moved* during exposure.' This was astonishing enough, but however skilled Mr. Snelling might be, I felt that the brief examination was insufficient; it must be as searching as it was possible to apply. So I talked the problem presented over with him, told him what I knew of the photographs, which was little enough then, and asked him to analyse the two negatives exhaustively at his leisure, to enlarge them so that any irregularities might be shown up and, in short, to break them down as faked work if it was possible to do so.

17

On calling a week later, as arranged, Snelling told me of his analysis and results. These can be summed up in the statement, which he made with emphasis, that both negatives were straight out-door shots and showed no trace of any faking process with which he was familiar. His first examination had been confirmed in all particulars and, on my pressing him further still, he declared that he would stake his reputation on the plates being unfaked, though, he added, they were not good ones, the first being a little over-exposed and the second badly under-exposed. '*I don't know anything about fairies,*' Snelling concluded, '*but these photographs are straight, open-air, single-exposure shots.*'

The instructions I then left with him were that the originals must be absolutely untouched; contact positives were to be made from them, and the negatives from these could be modified or strengthened to get good-class prints, but nothing more, no re-touching or treatments, and that two glass lantern-slides be made. It may be mentioned here that as soon as these copies had been made the original negatives were returned to me for safe keeping. They are still in my possession, as arrangements were made later with Mr. and Mrs. Wright to this effect. Mr. Snelling's opinion, written by himself, was given to me later, and a copy follows.

H. SNELLING,   *July 31, 1920*
    Photographer & Trade Enlarger,
      The Bridge, Wealdstone, Middx.

re Two Fairy Negatives

These two negatives are entirely genuine unfaked photographs of single exposure, open-air work, show movement in all the fairy figures, and there is no trace whatever of studio work involving card or paper models, dark backgrounds, painted figures, etc. In my opinion, they are both straight untouched pictures.

H. SNELLING

SIR ARTHUR CONAN DOYLE

On the strength of Snelling's analysis I ventured, a week or two afterwards, to show the slides to an audience at the Mortimer Halls, London, as a postscript to a lantern lecture I was giving there. I wanted to see for myself the photographs projected on the screen and hence greatly enlarged. They certainly looked extremely well, and many questions were asked. I explained that they were submitted as alleged photographs of fairies only; that I had no positive proof beyond the assurance of an expert photographer and, for the moment, merely wished to see them projected. The outcome of that brief view was that, through a mutual friend, news of the pictures reached Sir Arthur Conan Doyle and a letter I received soon after asked if it was true that I had 'fairy photographs' and, if so, could he see them or hear something about them. Correspondence led to a meeting and a discussion of the situation. Sir Arthur, I learnt, had arranged to supply an article to the *Strand Magazine* for its Christmas number, then seven months ahead, on 'Fairy Lore'. Hence, very naturally, his interest in possible photographs to illustrate it, especially when I showed him the beautiful prints that had been made—an interest that was increased when he examined the original negatives.

On hearing of Mr. Snelling's opinion, it was proposed, and agreed, that if the negatives survived a second expert's judgment, preferably Kodak's, then we should join forces and make the photographs a leading feature in the *Strand* article. Accordingly an appointment was made with Kodak's manager in Kingsway for the following week. We were received by Mr. West, the manager, and found that he had very kindly invited his studio chief and two other expert photographers to be present. The negatives were produced and examined by all at some length, and the results of the inspection and interview can be summed up as follows, all agreeing.

(1) The negatives are single exposure.
(2) The plates show no sign of being faked work, but that cannot be taken as conclusive evidence of genuineness.
(3) Kodak's were not willing to give any certificate concerning them because photography lent itself to a multitude of processes, and some clever operator *might* have made them artificially.
(4) The studio chief added that he thought the photographs might have been made by using the glen features and the girl as a background; then enlarging prints from these and painting in the figures; then taking half-plate and finally quarter-plate snaps, suitably lighted. All this, he agreed, would be clever work and take time.
(5) A remark made by one, as we were thanking them and bidding good-bye, was that 'after all, as fairies couldn't be true, the photographs must have been faked somehow.'

We came from Kodak's, therefore, without a certificate. The support given to Snelling's views was impressive but, by itself, it was not enough. The absence of any sign of faked work must be coupled with positive testimony on the personal side. Before we should be justified in accepting and sponsoring the 'event', it was clearly necessary for the family concerned, and all the circumstances to support the photography favourably, and indeed very adequately. It was decided, therefore, there and then that one of us should go to Yorkshire, interview the family and learn all that could be obtained on the spot. It was the month of July and, as Sir Arthur was off on an Australian tour in August, I undertook the task.

After our interview with Kodak's I confess I expected to find something much more elaborate than mere snapshots by a young girl. Questions had been pointed regarding the 'very appropriate' toadstools that appear on the bank and on one of which a fairy figure is poised; on the waterfall behind, which might well be a painted back-cloth; on the fact that the little girl standing in the stream was looking at the camera and not at the fairies; on the very conventional fairy figures themselves, just as one would have imagined them; and so on, in plenty. All of which meant that I might very well run into a clever frame-up if the photographs were faked work. So I went off to Bradford a few days later with a very open mind indeed. It had been arranged that Sir Arthur should hold up the story entirely till my investigation was concluded and then that it be abandoned failing very positive and satisfying evidence.

COTTINGLEY GLEN

From Bradford the tram takes one to Cottingley village, and I reached the address given at about three o'clock in the afternoon, Mrs. Wright having written that she and her husband would be pleased to meet me. Their cottage proved to be one that had its garden on the edge of a small valley stream, the 'beck' they called it, giving access to a glen of wild foliage running up to the moor. Mrs. Wright opened the door and, after introducing her daughter Elsie, a shy pretty girl of about sixteen, I explained something of my quest, and then, for an hour I heard of the incidents leading up to the photographs. All my queries were answered with willingness and candour.

The story ran thus. Three years earlier, in July 1917, a young cousin from South Africa had come to stay with the Wrights. This was Frances Griffiths, then ten years old. Mrs. Griffiths had come, too, to live with her sister, Mrs. Wright, while her husband was in France as a volunteer soldier of the South African contingent. The two girls, Elsie Wright and Frances Griffiths, then thirteen and ten years old, were thus together for the summer of 1917, and they spent most of their time in the beautiful glen at the back of the cottage. There they played, and repeatedly spoke of the fairies they met in the glen. The parents took little notice of this, and merely chaffed the children, thinking they imagined most of what they described.

Then it happened that Mr. Wright had a small camera, a Midg quarter-plate left with him by a relative, and he amused himself taking snaps and developing them in the scullery cupboard. It had been in use only about a month when, one day, it gave Elsie an idea. It was on a Saturday at the midday meal that there had been some bantering about 'the fairies' and Elsie retorted: 'Look here, Father, if you'll let me have your camera and tell me how it works I'll get a photo of the fairies. We've been playing with them this morning.' Mr. Wright laughed at them, and said he wasn't going to have his plates spoilt, and put them off. But the girls persisted and worried him, and at last he gave way. Putting one plate only in the box he set it, showed Elsie the trigger, and sent them off delighted. In less than an hour the girls were back and Elsie called out to her father, who was spending the Saturday afternoon in the garden, 'We've got the photo, I believe. Will you look?' Mr. Wright took the camera, saying he would see to it in the evening—and they had to be satisfied with that.

The story had got so far when Mr. Wright came in to his tea and, after introductions, we all sat down to this good Yorkshire meal together. I learnt then that Mr. Wright was the working manager of a small estate nearby, looked after an electrical plant, among other things, and generally attended to the outdoor work of the house there. Of the hearty Yorkshire type, of forthright speech and character, with a sense of humour and, like his wife, with a very cheerful disposition. Confirming the account of events so far, he then told me of his experience when developing the plate that evening three years earlier. With Elsie wedged in beside him in the small cupboard he put the plate in the dish, fully expecting only a blurr, and was startled to see flash up, almost at once, the dark figures which he took to be some white swans. Elsie saw them too, and hearing her father's exclamation shouted to Frances outside, 'We've got them; you'll see.' When the plate was finished Mr. Wright put it aside, saying they'd get a print in the morning and see what the swans looked like! Really uncertain as to what the children could have got hold of, as he told me, he took a sun-print in the morning with some curiosity, and was amazed at what he saw.

His questioning of the girls did not satisfy him, though they insisted that the figures in the photograph were the fairies they had so often described. Nothing would induce the children to give any other explanation, though the parents felt convinced that somehow they were being deceived. Mr. Wright told me at this point that neither he nor his wife had ever accepted the story given by the girls, notwithstanding that a month later they got the second photograph. So convinced, however, did Mr. Wright feel that the figures must be made of paper or the like that he went up the glen to the waterfall, which he recognised, and searched all about for scraps of paper cuttings. While the children were away he and his wife searched the girls' bedroom, too, for some sign as to the way it had been managed, but neither in the glen nor in the cottage could they discover anything. Not having found either of the girls untruthful, both were really concerned at the persistence with which they maintained their explanation—so the parents decided to let the matter alone. The camera was not loaned to the girls again, and beyond taking a few prints during the first weeks the two negatives were put away with some papers and books on a shelf and were there for three years—till Mrs. Wright happened to attend the local lecture referred to.

Elsie and I then walked up the glen that I might see the actual sites of the photographs and verify them, and I was glad of the opportunity of questioning the elder girl quietly by herself and of talking things over. We soon found the spots, and the surroundings were unmistakably the same as photographed. I was interested to notice several very large toadstools on the bank of the stream, and picked a couple to take home. Elsie explained where she knelt when taking

Photograph Number Three:

FRANCES AND THE LEAPING FAIRY

Photograph taken in August 1920. Camera, the Cameo Quarter.

This negative, and those known as Numbers 4 and 5, were as strictly examined as the earlier, and similarly disclose no trace of being other than perfectly genuine photographs. They all proved also to have been taken from the packet given to the girls, each plate of which had been privately marked by the manufacturers. The fairy is leaping up from the leaves below and hovering for a moment—it had done so three or four times. Rising a little higher than before, Frances thought it would touch her face, and involuntarily tossed her head back. The fairy's light covering appears to be close fitting: the wings were lavender in colour.

Frances and the group of dancing fairies and, while we were there, I asked why Frances was not looking at the fairies instead of gazing at the camera. The reply was: 'Why, Frances wanted me to take her photograph directly we got out of the garden, she was crazy for it; I said we might just as well take her with the fairies— so she had to wait!' A curious explanation this will appear to most, as it did to me, but there it was. Frances, apparently, was much more interested in the camera that they had for the first time than she was in dancing fairies she could see any day, and from her point of view I suppose it was understandable. This answer of Elsie's is typical of the simplicity I met with throughout the investigation. Indeed, that which impressed me most in our conversation was the utter unconcernedness of Elsie at the affair being anything special. She had seen and played with fairy creatures since she could remember anything, and actually to photograph them did not appeal to her as being very extraordinary. I might mention here, though I will deal with it more adequately later, that both the girls were good simple clairvoyants, quite unspoilt because unaware of it. They had the advantage, also, of being able to see only the subtler physical region and not anything beyond, their extra-sensory perception being strictly limited; hence there was very little confusion or distortion in the focus of their clairvoyance.

As we discussed the incidents again that evening, both Mr. and Mrs. Wright were amazed indeed when I told them, for the first time, of the experts' reports on the two negatives. 'Why,' exclaimed Mr. Wright, 'it looks as if they might be real after all!' I ventured then on the use Sir Arthur Conan Doyle proposed to make of the photographs, but at once they all demurred. They felt it as a real difficulty, and it took all I could do by way of persuasion to obtain their consent to the publication. One condition was insisted on—that their proper names should not be printed, nor the name of the village. I would very much rather have had permission to give the correct names and all particulars, but I had to be content with the conditions made. I suggested then a money payment, as Sir Arthur had wished this, but Mr. Wright declined very firmly, almost indignantly, saying that if the photographs *were* genuine then they shouldn't be soiled by being paid for!

Conning over the position in my hotel at Bradford, for I was spending some time in the neighbourhood, I had to admit that the two probable motives for fraudulent work, namely, money and notoriety, were obviously quite absent. It is but fair, too, that I should give my testimony here to Mr. and Mrs. Wright's sincerity and candour and, in my opinion, their absolute honesty. If any fraudulent intent and purpose whatever lay behind these photographs it was not, I was satisfied, within their knowledge. And that view, I had to allow, cut out any likelihood, almost the possibility, of fraud, because of Mr. Wright's own testimony to the circumstances of the first photograph. The loading of the camera with the single plate, the time the girls were away, the development of the plate by himself

23

that evening, the inability of any of the family to devise photographic trickery—all these facts seemed entirely to favour a genuine happening, however unique and strange. Yet such an event as fairy photographs needed to be supported by evidence as incontrovertible as it was possible to obtain. So at my last visit to the Wright family on that trip I made a further suggestion.

COULD MORE PHOTOGRAPHS BE TAKEN?

One explanation, other than the motives of money and fame, was conceivable, however unlikely. This was to assume that the children had been the tool of someone skilled in photographic work who, in some way, had substituted a plate for the one that had been put in the Midg. This would mean that the girls had been party to a fraud and, having started with falsehoods, did not like to withdraw and own up when seriously questioned. A far-fetched suggestion, perhaps, in the circumstances; later, however, some critics actually advanced this theory that I then foresaw as just a possibility, a possibility which we should be wise to disprove if it could be done. Nothing, it seemed to me, could be so conclusive as more photographs, with provision against such substitution.

The suggestion I made, therefore, was that Frances should come and stay at Cottingley during her August holidays and the girls, now sixteen and thirteen years old, should try for more. Mr. and Mrs. Griffiths had fortunately remained in England after the war and were within reach on the east coast. Mr. and Mrs. Wright readily consented and, on arriving in London, I wrote to Mrs. Griffiths and proposed running up to see them at Scarborough.

THE TWO FAIRY PHOTOGRAPHS AND THE *Strand Magazine*

It was the eve, almost, of Sir Arthur's trip to Australia. He and I went over all the material I had to report and we agreed that the analysis of the photographs, coupled, as it was now, with satisfactory testimony on the personal side, justified publishing the article and the pictures in the *Strand*. The contract, therefore, was completed with the *Strand* Editor, and we both undertook to keep silence concerning the whole affair until after the magazine was on sale the following December. I promised, of course, to send word to Sydney should we have any success with our new venture in the Cottingley glen. This was early August 1920, and I arranged to go north again, as Mrs. Griffiths had written favourably of the suggestion that Frances should visit Cottingley later in the month.

THREE MORE PHOTOGRAPHS

Two good quarter-plate cameras were bought, one for each of the girls, and then I went to Illingworth's factory for the supply of two dozen plates. I saw the manager and explained that I wanted him to be able to check and verify the plates if I brought them back after their use. How they were marked only he and his workman must know. This was promised, and the following day I had the twenty-four plates all privately marked and re-wrapped.

The trip to Scarborough proved satisfactory. I interviewed Mrs. Griffiths and Frances, both then seen for the first time, and a half-hour's talk with Frances explained a good deal. The girl, at that time thirteen years old, was mediumistic, which merely means that she had loosely knit ectoplasmic material in her body. The subtle ectoplasmic or etheric material of the body, which with most people is very closely interwoven with the denser frame, was in her case unlocked or, rather, loosened, and on seeing her I had the first glimpse of how the nature spirits had densified their own normal bodies sufficiently to come into the field of the camera's range. This explanation emerged more fully later, however. For the moment I was concerned wholly with the practical arrangements which would enable us to get, if possible, that further evidence which would, this time, be un-assailable. Frances was delighted with the invitation she had received from her aunt, Mrs. Wright, and in the middle of August she went off to Cottingley to spend the second fortnight of her school holidays there with Elsie.

I went off, too, to Cottingley again, taking the two cameras and plates from London, and met the family and explained to the two girls the simple working of the cameras, giving one to each to keep. The cameras were loaded, and my final advice was that they need go up to the glen only on fine days as they had been accustomed to do before and 'tice the fairies, as they called their way of attracting them, and see what they could get. I suggested only the most obvious and easy precautions about lighting and distance, for I knew it was essential they should feel free and unhampered and with no burden of responsibility. If nothing came of it all I told them, they were not to mind a bit.

Often I have been asked why I didn't stay with them and see the attempt through. The answer is, unfortunately, not convincing to everybody, but those who have some knowledge of the habits of the nature spirits will admit its validity. Had I been present it is exceedingly unlikely that anything would have presented itself to be photographed. The fact is, as the girls themselves knew well, that the fairy life will not 'come out' from the shrubs and plants around unless the human visitor is of a sympathetic quality. Such a visitor needs to be not merely sympathe-tic in mentality, for that is of little use; he must have a warm emotional sympathy, childlike in its innocence and simplicity. The girls thought I might get used to the fairies, or rather, they to me, in a month or two, but I had my doubts whether I could cultivate the necessary quality even in that time. At any rate, it was no good attempting it then.

Bidding good-bye, I returned home. Then, during that second fortnight in August 1920, it rained almost continuously throughout the country. The papers reported the rain as general, and I was much afraid that even a visit up to the glen could not comfortably have been made, since the foliage was so thick. But just as the fortnight ended I had a letter from Elsie to say that Frances had gone back to Scarborough that day. They had been able to go up to the glen only on two occasions when, in the afternoon of two days, the sun had shone. On the first visit they had taken two snaps and on the second one only. (Photographs Numbers 3, 4 and 5.) The three negatives were sent with the letter, which had added: 'Afraid they are not very good, but two are fairly clear.' The two 'clear' ones were of the fairy poised on the bush leaves offering a posy to Elsie, and the leaping fairy in front of Frances. The third had features that I could see would be very valuable for testing, as it was a dense mix-up of grasses and harebells with intertwined figures and faces. The results of their two trips seemed to promise exceedingly well.

With the photographs I called at Illingworth's and saw the manager. He took them in to the factory to examine them and presently returned to say, 'Yes, these three plates are from the parcel you had from us.' The manager was particularly interested in the third negative. He would not commit himself to any opinion on the first two, but the third be described as 'an impossibility to fake.' At least I had the proof that the three plates were from the number supplied to the girls.

These negatives were then subjected to the same rigorous analysis that the two earlier had survived. They also were greatly enlarged to check consistency in lighting; for any sign of the grain of paper, canvas or paint or anything that could have been used to represent fairy figures. Also, concerning the leaping fairy, the search was exhaustive to find the thread 'supporting the figure'. Nothing whatever came of all this that indicated anything amiss. One point made was that the figures themselves were rather stronger than the rest and I was reminded of Arthur Wright's remark that the dark patches flashed up directly he put the plate in the developer. The explanation of this seems to be that the fairy bodies are slightly self-luminous, a fact supported in subsequent investigations.

Again I visited Cottingley and learnt all that Elsie had to tell of the fortnight with Frances, and this was mostly of her disappointment in not being able to get up to the glen more often because of the weather. The afternoon that the first two photographs were taken the girls were gone about an hour and a half, Mrs. Wright told me. Elsie was very matter of fact about them and described one or two features in answer to my questions. The leaping fairy, she said, jumped up several times in front of Frances and then, 'when I took the snap it jumped so near her face she tossed her head back and nearly spoilt it all!' The third picture was quite a chance shot; it was taken among the grasses at the fringe of a pool near the beck. They had seen some movements in the long grasses and one tallish figure, and took a snap and hoped for the best. It was indeed fortunate that they did, for in this last photograph there are quite a number of faces and figures that can be traced in the tangle. It was this one that intrigued the photographic experts so much. The cocoon in the middle, with the fairy seated in it, was new to the girls; they did not know what it was. It was not until my later interviews with fairy lovers in the New Forest that I had the explanation of this given to me, as a special restorative vessel used after lengthy spells of dull and misty weather— a fairy-bath, they called it.

When the photographic analysis and this further personal visit were completed, I wrote at length to Sir Arthur in Australia with a full account of the happenings. A cordial reply came in due course and this confirmed my suggestion that nothing should be told of this later success till after the Christmas number of the *Strand* was out. It was arranged for the corroborative evidence, with copies of the new photographs, to be published in the *Strand Magazine* for March 1921.

A Straightforward Narrative

In the foregoing statement I have confined myself to the immediate steps taken to verify or disprove the authenticity of the Cottingley fairy photographs. The reader has here a narrative of the gathering of evidence from the photographic examination and from the personal interviews with the Wright family and Frances, and with these essentials before him he can form his own conclusions. It is not easy to convey the sense of integrity I felt at the end of the investigation; to share it properly one would have to meet the parents and the children as I did. Here I can only register my own personal conversion to the acceptance of the five photographs as genuine in every sense of the word. It took a great deal of time and concentrated attention to convince me, but I can claim that the inquiry was thorough.

Later Corroborations

Among the many incidents of a corroborative character that occurred later were the following, which will serve to conclude this first part of the story.

THE PRESS—Following the publication of the article in the *Strand* in December 1920, many enquiries were made as to who were the children concerned and where was the 'fairy glen'? Our promise to the family had meant that Yorkshire was the only indication that was given in the article, but this proved to be sufficient for the *Daily News & Westminster Gazette*. They commissioned one of their reporters, a Yorkshire man, to search the country and discover the truth; 'to break the fraud', I learnt afterwards was the way they put it to him. The first I knew of this was when, one day in January, this gentleman called on me, introduced himself, and then frankly told me he was making no headway. Asked as to what had happened, he said that, knowing Yorkshire well and the Bradford district particularly, he had started there and had fortunately, through some local rumour, soon discovered the family at Cottingley. He then had interviewed the father, mother, and the daughter separately. Also he had seen and verified the

Photograph Number Four:

FAIRY OFFERING A POSY TO ELSIE

The fairy is standing almost still, poised on the bush leaves. The wings were shot with yellow. An interesting point is shown in this photograph: Elsie is not looking directly at the sprite. The reason seems to be that the human eye is disconcerting. If the fairy be actively moving it does not matter much, but if motionless and aware of being gazed at then the nature spirit will usually withdraw and apparently vanish. With fairy lovers the habit of looking at first a little sideways is common.

glen sites. Photographic establishments in Bradford and the district around had been visited and many other possible sources of information—but nothing came of it all. Friends of the Wright family had been questioned, enquiries were made in all directions; indeed, he had evidently done his best and could find nothing even suspicious. It all appeared straightforward and, as he put it, 'too simple to break'. I then told him something of my own lengthy efforts and he laughingly declared on parting that he was very nearly believing in fairies himself! The next day, and again the week following, very fair and interesting reports were printed of his adventures in Yorkshire, giving the full names and all particulars this time, and concluding with the admission that no flaw had been found. (See the *Westminster Gazette,* January 12th and 21st, 1921.)

A LANTERN LECTURE—In many towns in England and Scotland, during 1921, I gave a lecture upon fairies, illustrated with lantern slides, and one evening was in the town hall of a city in the Midlands. The large building was filled, and when the chairman and I stepped on the platform I was much interested to see the enormous screen provided for the lantern projection: it spread over the whole end of the hall behind the stage. A glance at the gallery at the back showed a lantern overhanging the audience the size of which I had never seen before—it resembled a naval gun—so I anticipated a fine projection and was not disappointed. The fairy photographs, as also many of parts of the glen, showed up magnificently, particularly the group of dancing fairies in front of Frances, and the leaping sprite. These had to be shown again. With the lecture finished, the lantern operator came along with my box of slides and handing them to me he said, 'Can I have a word?' We went aside and he then explained that the lantern used was a very special one and, among other purposes, it was used to check up suspected signatures, money documents, alleged forgeries, and so on. Then he added, smiling, 'Some of us were sure your photographs were faked and that when the first one came up the fake would be shown up all round—and you'd clear! The boys up in the gallery were all ready for it, but we were done. Those photographs are straight; nothing else could have stood up to that lantern. Looks as if I had to believe in fairies!'

FRANCES IN SOUTH AFRICA—Early in 1923 a copy of the well-known paper in South Africa, the *Cape Argus,* dated November 25th, 1922, was sent to me. It contained a whole page-wide heading:

CAPE TOWN LINK IN WORLD CONTROVERSY
STARTLING SEQUEL TO AN *ARGUS* ARTICLE
REMARKABLE LETTER IN SUPPORT OF SIR A. C. DOYLE

The substance of the five-column article that followed was a letter that little Frances had written from England away back in November 1918, just before the Armistice, to a friend in Woodstock, Cape Town. The letter was reproduced in

Photograph Number Five:

FAIRIES AND THEIR SUN-BATH

This is especially remarkable as it contains a feature quite unknown to the girls. The sheath or cocoon appearing in the middle of the grasses had not been seen by them before, and they had no idea what it was. Fairy observers of Scotland and the New Forest, however, were familiar with it and described it as a magnetic bath, woven very quickly by the fairies and used after dull weather, in the autumn especially. The interior seems to be magnetised in some manner that stimulates and pleases.

the *Argus* in facsimile, to prove the childish writing, as fortunately the young friend, a Miss Parvin, had kept it, together with the print Frances had enclosed with it. The letter from Frances ran thus:

> '. . . all think the war will be over in a few days, we are going to get our flags to hang up in our bedroom. I am sending you two photos, both of me, one is me in a bathing costume in our back yard, uncle Arthur took that, while the other is me with some fairies up the beck, Elsie took that one. Rosebud is as fat as ever and I have made her some new clothes. How are Teddy and dolly?'

On the back of the print of the fairies dancing in front of herself she wrote: 'Elsie and I are very friendly with the beck fairies. . . .'

This letter, which was produced by Miss Parvin at the *Cape Argus* office, was described by the interviewer for the paper as 'written in indelible pencil and was just so much faded as to bear every appearance of having been written four years ago.' The *Argus* proceeds to comment:

> 'The plain fact surely is that, however sceptical you may be about the existence of fairies, the production of this letter written by Frances Griffiths, a former Cape Town girl, to Johanna Parvin, at Woodstock, in November 1918, is a valuable piece of evidence in support of Sir A. C. Doyle's story. And for this reason. It was not until 1920 that this photograph began to attract attention. Yet for two years before Sir Arthur had seen this photograph, a similar photograph had been lying at Woodstock, Cape Town, sent from one girl friend to another with far less comment than was displayed in writing about their several dolls! . . . Isn't the very intimate and insignificant detail of it, the very off-hand manner in which a world phenomenon is dismissed in a couple of lines—isn't all this the best kind of evidence possible that, two years before Conan Doyle ever started this controversy, Frances Griffiths believed implicitly in the existence of fairies: so implicitly indeed as to discuss them with no more surprise or emphasis than she discussed her dad, her dolls, and the war?'

The *Argus* had published a review of Sir A. Conan Doyle's book, *The Coming of the Fairies*, previously: it was this that had been seen by Frances' friend, Miss Parvin. The *Argus* concludes this report of Frances' letter of 1918 by adding some questions on its own account, thus: 'Although we think it only fair and proper that this evidence should be brought to light . . . the following points still stand as a hindrance to our acceptance . . .' and then follow four or five very pertinent and reasonable queries. As these have been raised, too, by others, I will give here what I believe to be correct replies, so far as I am able.

Question: Why did the **photographs** suddenly cease after the three additional ones obtained in 1920?

Answer: First, it appears to have been necessary for the two girls to be together. Both were good simple clairvoyants, and Frances was a good medium for the provision of the ectoplasmic and denser material needed to enable the nature spirits to materialise their forms. Clairvoyance and this mediumistic quality are not necessarily found in the same person, though they sometimes are, as in the case of Frances. In 1921, that is the year later, during the summer I took the greatest pains to secure more photographs. The girls were together again in the glen, and the conditions seemed to be precisely as they had been previously— but though the nature spirits would 'come out' and approach the girls, they would not use Frances' aura to strengthen their forms. With a sort of gesture of dislike they retreated almost at once. Now that, strictly, is all I can say about it. My surmise, which I conveyed to Sir Arthur, was that the attainment of puberty quite probably was the reason for the failure to get photographs. Sufficiently dense material of a suitable nature was not to be had or, rather, was unacceptable— and I must leave it at that.

Question: Why—if 'the processes of puberty are often fatal to psychic power'— (which is Conan Doyle's explanation of the cessation of the photographs) does his book then tell of a number of married women who say they have seen fairies?

Answer: The *Argus* here assumes that clairvoyance and mediumistic ability are the same thing. That is not so. Though they occasionally are found together, this is not always the case. Frances was clairvoyant within very narrow limits, but she was exceptionally good in her mediumship and quite unspoilt. To take her auric material, or ectoplasm, to densify their bodies was very evidently a delightful sensation for the nature spirits. The fairies had probably done this often, before the camera was used at all. The tangible and concrete clarity of shape and outline obtained was evidently an enjoyable experience, resembling a stimulating bathe. It was while using her aura that the forms came within the optical field of the camera, as they were then much denser than their normal structure. From one or two chance contacts I made myself when near Frances, I am fairly sure that the fairies dancing could actually have been seen by many had it been possible to be near. The clairvoyance of both Elsie and Frances was another matter altogether and was due to the use of their etheric eyes. They continued to see the fairies even when photography was no longer possible. Everyone possesses these etheric eyes: they resemble concave discs behind and around the eyeball, something like a saucer shade behind an electric bulb. The etheric discs endow the physical eyes with vitality and fire, but normally do not function independently. As a child I suffered a good deal myself from their activity, but fortunately grew out of it. When they do function, etheric sight is exercised and about another octave of light, more or less, becomes consciously objective. This independent activity of the etheric eyes, when it occurs, may be under some control or none. When uncontrolled, as in my own case in childhood, it can be the cause of much fear and distress, for the things seen are seldom understood. When under control, though this may be almost unconscious control, as it was with Elsie and Frances, then, provided the range be limited, a thrilling extension of vision dawns. Such is a brief description of etheric sight and the type of clairvoyance that, within rather well-defined limits, both these girls possessed. And Frances, in addition, had a beautifully clear, yet loosely knit, etheric aura, yielding easily accessible ectoplasmic material, which was acceptable to the nature spirits up to her thirteenth year.

Question: In the photograph of the gnome-like creature, Elsie's hand is either distorted or abnormal: what is wrong with it?

Answer: On my very first meeting with Elsie, her hands attracted attention and, later in the evening, I remarked on the gnome photograph and asked to examine her hand. Very slender and with exceptionally long fingers, the hand, when extended, was abnormal, though not so much as to be unsightly. With her permission I took a pencil outline of the hand and fingers, extended flat on a sheet of paper, and they proved to be a good deal longer than the average. The appearance of dislocation at the wrist that some have remarked, I cannot explain, except as a result of foreshortening and movement.

Question: Why hasn't anybody else in the world ever been able to photograph fairies but Frances Griffiths and Elsie Wright?

Answer: This was the last question on the *Argus* list, and I can only suggest the rarity of the combination which, apparently by chance, succeeded at Cottingley. It is not, however, the case that no one else has been able to get anything at all of the same character. Several other photographs exist, and two or three were reproduced in Sir A. C. Doyle's book, *The Coming of the Fairies*—but they are in quite another category in terms of clarity and definition. I have to agree that the Cottingley photographs are at present, so far as I know, unique in being the most definite and vivid record so far obtained of this type of natural phenomena.

PART II

CLAIRVOYANT INVESTIGATIONS

A friend, Mr. Geoffrey Hodson, has helped me many a time with his expert clairvoyance in the subtle field above the limits of physical sight, which is the field of activity of the nature spirits, and, when we were working together a few years ago, he made interesting notes of his observations on the growth of plants. In the summary of these notes that is given below the word 'etheric' is used to denote the field of electro-magnetic activity, now known to be the medium through which so many bio-chemical transformations take place.

When examining bulbs growing in bowls, large numbers of small microscopic etheric creatures are to be seen moving about in and around the growing plants. They are visible at the etheric level as points of light playing around the stem and passing in and out of the bulb. They have power to rise into the air around to a height about equal in that of the plant: they absorb something from the atmosphere, re-enter the tissues and discharge it. This process goes on continuously. The creatures are entirely self-absorbed, sufficiently self-conscious to experience a dim sense of well-being and to feel affection for the plant, which they regard as their body; they have no consciousness apart from this. When outside the plant and absorbing what seems to be a charge of energy, they become enlarged and look like pale violet and lilac-coloured spheres about two inches in diameter. Having expanded to the largest size of which they are capable they return, enter the plant and discharge the vital force which they have absorbed. In addition to this the plants themselves, on their own, can be seen to take in a certain amount. There is also a natural vital flow from the half-grown plants upwards to about two feet above them, and in this other tiny creatures play and dance. To focused etheric sight these are less than a quarter of an inch in size, and are also spherical. The little nature spirits apparently do not confine their work to one plant or even to one bowl—for they flit about from one to another if the bowls are near each other. The bulbs themselves give the impression of being small power-houses, each charged with potent vitality. The etheric colour of the bulb when growing is pinkish-violet, with an intenser light in the centre, and from this centre rises an upward flowing etheric stream, carrying with it, at a slower pace, both moisture and nutriment.

As a result of observations and attempts to understand the processes of growth, Mr. Hodson came to the following conclusions:

In the heart of every seed is a living, quiescent, centre which contains the stored-up results of the previous season as a vibratory possibility. Apparently the awakening or stirring to life in an appropriate soil produces a subtle equivalent to sound. This 'sound' then seems to be heard in the elemental regions around and the nature spirit builders answer the call. Every type of growth—stem, shoot, leaf and flower—appears to have its own note or call, to which the appropriate builder responds. As sound itself has a form-producing effect, it is probably the means by which the archetypal form of the plant, latent in the seed and in the minds of a superior order of nature spirits, is projected to the etheric level as a patterned shape. Some of the results of this vibratory call from the seed appear to be:

34

(1) to separate and insulate the atmosphere around the seed;

(2) to set the matter within the isolated space vibrating at the required rate, and to specialise it in readiness for the work of the builders;

(3) to call the builders, who, entering the specialised sphere, are then able to materialise themselves down to the level at which they have to work;

(4) probably also to assist in shaping the latent pattern of the plant and so to have a guide, a ground-plan, ready for the little builders.

Different vibrational 'calls' arise as stem, shoot, leaf and flower have in turn to be built and the corresponding builder then arrives to work on its own appropriate task.

The subtle sound appears to radiate not only from the life centre of the seed, but also from every embryo cell as each develops; the builder concerned with that cell absorbs the material required—that which responds to the same vibration as himself and the cell he is building—and transforms it by changing it from free to specialised material and then passes it to the cell from which the sound is uttered and builds it piecemeal into the etheric pattern. The cell is thus gradually nourished and enlarged till it reaches its proper limit, then it divides and the process is repeated. While the material is in close association with the builder, it is not only specialised to suit the growing cell, it is also coloured by adopting the vibratory rate of the tiny nature spirit concerned.

Each change in structure and colour seems to call for another group of builders for when the flower-bud stage is approached a new set arrives on the scene. These use a more conscious technique, though they work in precisely the same way. When the flower itself is to be built the fairies proper appear and they are responsible for all the colouring and the exquisite structures of the flowers. The flower fairies are sufficiently conscious of their special work to take, apparently, a keen pleasure in its performance. They remain in close attendance as each bud and petal develops and appear to be appreciative of human admiration; this is probably due to their ability to respond to emotion. When flowers are cut the fairy-builders may accompany the blooms and stay with them for some time.

When the completely flowered condition is reach a full chord is sounding; for those who hear this, gardens have an additional joy, though for many it can be contacted only as a scent.*

This summary of some of Mr. Hodson's notes shows how very complicated are the activities we are accustomed to sum up so tersely as 'natural'.

IN THE GLEN

In 1921, the year after the second set of photographs had been obtained, as I

* *Fairies at Work and Play*, by G. Hodson, Theosophical Publishing House, London.

have already mentioned, we were again attempting to get further photographic evidence. In addition to this I was anxious to check the clairvoyant ability of the girls, so I persuaded Mr. and Mrs. Geoffrey Hodson to spend a few days with us in the Cottingley district. This they very kindly did, and though the photographic attempts failed in that year many joint observations were made and my purpose in this connection was in a large measure achieved. Mr. Hodson had a wider and more trained vision than either Elsie or Frances and he explored the glen with them and made notes of what they all saw. These notes were supplied to Sir Arthur Conan Doyle, and as the material is very much to the point some of it is given in detail here.

Seated in Cottingley Glen with the girls Mr. Hodson saw all they saw, and more. He would point in a certain direction and ask them for a description of what they saw, and this he always obtained correctly, within the limits of their powers. The whole glen, according to his account, was swarming with many forms of elemental life, and he saw not only wood-elves, gnomes, and goblins, but the rarer undines, floating in the stream. Something of what they saw is shown in the following extracts from his somewhat disjointed notes.

Gnomes and Fairies. 'In the field we saw figures about the size of the gnome. They were making weird grimaces and grotesque contortions at the group. One in particular took great delight in knocking his knees together. These forms appeared to Elsie singly, one dissolving and another appearing in its place. I, however, saw them in a group, with one figure more prominently visible than the rest. Elsie also saw a gnome like the one in the photograph, but not so bright, and not coloured. I saw a group of female figures playing a game somewhat resembling the children's game of oranges-and-lemons. They played in a ring, and the game then resembled the grand chain in the lancers. One fairy stood more or less motionless in the centre of the ring while the remainder, who appeared to be decked with flowers and to show colours not normally their own, danced round her. Some next joined hands and made an archway for the others, who moved in and out as in a maze. I noticed that the result of the game appeared to be the forming of a vortex of force, which streamed upwards to a distance of about four or five feet from the ground. I also noticed that in those parts of the field where the grass was thicker and darker there appeared to be correspondingly extra activity among the fairy creatures.'

Water Nymphs. 'In the beck itself, near the large rock, at a slight fall in the water, I saw a water sprite. It was an entirely nude female figure with long fair hair, which it appeared to be combing or passing through its fingers. I was not sure whether it had any feet or not. Its form was of a dazzling rosy whiteness, and its face very beautiful. The arms, which were long and graceful, were moved with a wave-like motion. It sometimes appeared to be singing, though I could hear no sound. It was in a kind of cave formed by a projecting piece of rock and

36

some moss. Apparently it had no wings, and it moved with a sinuous, almost snake-like, motion, in a semi-horizontal position. Its atmosphere and feeling were quite different from those of the fairies. It showed no consciousness of my presence, and though I waited with my camera in the hope of snapping it, it did not detach itself from its surroundings, in which it was in some way merged.'

Wood Elves. '(Under the old beeches in the wood, Cottingley, August 12, 1921.) Two tiny wood elves came racing over the ground past us as we sat on a fallen tree trunk. Seeing us, they pulled up short about five feet away, and stood regarding us with considerable amusement but no fear. They appeared as if completely covered in a tight-fitting one-piece skin, which shone slightly as if wet. They had hands and feet large and out of proportion to their bodies. Their legs were somewhat thin; ears large and almost pear-shaped, pointed upwards. Their noses appeared almost pointed and their mouths wide. No teeth and no structure inside the mouth, not even a tongue, so far as I could see. It was as if the whole was made up of a piece of jelly. Surrounding them as an etheric double surrounds a physical form is a greenish light something like chemical vapour. As Frances came up and sat within a foot of them they withdrew, as if in alarm, to a distance of eight feet or so, where they remained apparently regarding us and comparing notes of their impressions. These two live in the roots of a large beech tree; they disappeared through a crevice into which they walked as one might do into a cave, and sank below the ground.'

Water Fairy. '(August 14, 1921.) By a small waterfall, which threw up a fine spray, was seen poised in the spray a diminutive fairy form of an exceedingly tenuous nature. It appeared to have two main colourings, the upper part of its body and aura being pale violet, the lower part pale pink. This colouring appeared to penetrate right through aura and denser body, the outline of the latter merging into the former. This creature hung poised, its body curved gracefully backwards, its left arm held high above its head, as if upheld by the vital force in the spray, much as a seagull supports itself against the wind. It was human in shape but did not show any characteristics of sex. It was lying on its back in a curved position against the flow of the stream. It remained motionless in this attitude for some moments, then flashed out of view. I did not notice any wings.'

Fairies, Elves, Gnomes, and a Brownie. '(Sunday, August 14, 9 p.m., in the field.) Lovely, still, moonlight night. The field appears to be densely populated with nature spirits of various kinds—a brownie, fairies, eleves, and gnomes.

Brownie. 'He is rather taller than the normal, say eight inches, dressed entirely in brown with facings of a darker shade, bag-shaped cap, almost conical, knee-breeches, stockings, and has thin ankles, and large pointed feet like gnomes' feet. He stands facing us, in no way afraid, perfectly friendly and much interested; he gazes wide-eyed at us, with a curious expression as of dawning intellect. It is as if he were reaching after something just beyond his mental grasp. He looks

37

behind him at a group of fairies who are approaching us and moves to one side as if to make way. His mental attitude is semi-dreamlike, as of a child who would say, "I can stand and watch this all day without being tired." He clearly sees much of our auras and is strongly affected by our emanations.

Fairies. 'Frances sees tiny fairies dancing in a circle, the figures gradually expanding in size till they reach eighteen inches, the ring widening in proportion. Elsie sees a vertical circle of dancing fairies flying slowly round; as each one touches the grass he appears to perform a few quick steps and then continue his slow motion round the circle. The fairies who are dancing have long skirts, through which their limbs can be seen; viewed astrally, the circle is bathed in golden yellow light, with the outer edges of many hues, violet predominating. The movement of the fairies is reminiscent of that of the great wheel at Earls Court. The fairies float very slowly, remaining motionless as far as bodies and limbs are concerned, until they come round to the ground again. There is a tinkling music accompanying all this. It appears to have more of the aspect of a ceremony than a game. Frances sees two fairy figures performing as if on the stage, one with wings, one without. Their bodies shine with the effect of rippling water in the sun. The fairy without wings has bent over backwards like a contortionist till its head touches the ground, while the winged figure bends over it. Frances sees a small Punch-like figure, with a kind of Welsh hat, doing a sort of dancing by striking its heel on the ground, and at the same time raising its hat and bowing. Elsie sees fairy flower, like a carnation in shape, the head appearing where the stalk touches the flower and the green sepals forming a tunic from which the arms protrude, while the petals form a skirt, below which are rather thin legs. It is tripping across the grass. Its colouring is pink like a carnation, in a pale, suffused kind of way. I see couples a foot high, female and male, dancing in a slow waltz-like motion in the middle of the field. They appear even to reverse. They are clothed in etheric matter and are rather ghostlike in appearance. Their bodies are outlined with grey light and show little detail.

'Elsie sees a small imp reminiscent of a monkey, revolving slowly round a stalk to the top of which he is clinging. He has an impish face, and is looking our way as if performing for our benefit.

'The brownie appears during all this to have taken upon himself the duties of showman. I see what may be described as a fairy fountain about twenty feet ahead. It is caused by an uprush of fairy force from the ground, spreading fishtail fashion higher into the air; it is many-hued. This is also seen by Frances.'

'(Monday, August 15, in the field.) I saw three figures racing across the field towards the wood, the same figures previously seen in the wood. When at a distance of about ten yards from the wall they leapt over it into the wood and disappeared. Elsie sees in the centre of the field a very beautiful fairy figure somewhat resembling Mercury, without winged sandals, but with fairy wings.

Nude; light curly hair, kneeling down in a clump of grass, with its attention fixed on something in the ground. It changes its position; first it is sitting back on its heels, and then it is rising to its full kneeling height. Much larger than usual, probably eighteen inches. It moves its arms over some object on the ground. It has picked up something from the ground (I think a baby) and holds it to its breast and seems to be praying. Has Greek features and resembles a Greek statue; like a figure out of a Greek tragedy.'

Fairies. '(Tuesday, August 16, 10 p.m., in the field, by the light of a small photographic lamp.) Elsie sees a circle of fairies tripping round, hands joined, facing outwards. A figure appears in the centre of the ring; at the same time the fairies face inwards.'

Goblins. 'A group of goblins came running towards us from the wood to within fifteen feet of us. They differ somewhat from the wood elves, having more the look of gnomes, though they are smaller, being about the size of small brownies.'

Fairy. 'Elsie sees a beautiful fairy quite near; it is nude, with golden hair, and is kneeling in the grass, looking this way, with hands on knees, smiling at us. It has a very beautiful face, and is concentrating its gaze on me. This figure came within five feet of us, and after being described faded away.'

Elf. 'Elsie sees a kind of elf who seems to be going so fast that it blows his hair back. One can sense the wind round him, yet he is stationary, though he appears to be busy hurrying along.'

Goblins. 'Elsie sees a flight of little mannikins, imp-like in appearance, descending slantwise on to the grass. They form into two lines which cross each other as they come down. One line is coming down vertically, feet touching head, the other comes across them, shoulder to shoulder. On reaching the ground they all run off in different directions, all serious, as if intent upon some business. The elves from the wood appear to be chiefly engaged in racing across the field, though no purpose seems to be served by their speed or presence. Few of them pass near us without pulling up to stare. The elves seem to be the most curious of all the fairy creatures. Frances sees three and calls them goblins.'

Blue Fairy. 'A fairy with wings and general colouring of sea blue and pale pink. The wings are webbed, and marked in varying colours like those of a butterfly. The form is perfectly modelled and practically nude. A golden star shines in the hair.'

Fairy Band. 'There has suddenly arrived in the field a fairy director with a band of fairy people. Their arrival causes a bright radiance to shine in the field, visible to us sixty yards away. The director is very autocratic and definite in her orders, holding unquestioned command. The band spread themselves out into a gradually widening circle around her, and as they do so a soft glow spreads over the grass.

39

They are actually vivifying and stimulating the growth in the field. This is a moving band which arrived in this field swinging high over the tree-tops as if from a considerable distance. Inside a space of two minutes the circle has spread to approximately twelve feet wide and is wonderfully radiant with light. Each member of the band is linked to the leader by a thin stream of light. These streams are of different colours, though chiefly yellow, deepening to orange. They meet in the centre of the circle, merging in her aura, and there is a constant flow backwards and forwards among them. The form produced by this is something like an inverted fruit dish, with the central fairy as the stem, and the lines of light which flow in a graceful even curve forming the sides of the bowl. This band is in intense activity, as if it had much to do and little time in which to do it. The director is vivified and instructed from within herself and appears to have her consciousness seated upon a more subtle plane than that upon which she is working.'

Fairies. 'Elsie sees a tall and stately fairy come across the field to a clump of harebells. It is carrying in its arms something which may be a baby fairy, wrapped in gauzy substance. It lays this in the clump of harebells and kneels down as though stroking something, and after a time fades away. We catch impressions of four-footed creatures being ridden by winged figures who are thin and bent over their mounts like jockeys. It is no known animal which they bestride, having a face something like that of a caterpillar.

'Amongst this fairy activity, which appears all over the field, one glimpses an occasional gnome-like form walking with serious mien across the field, whilst the wood-elves and other imp-like forms run about amongst their more seriously employed fairy-kind. All three of us keep seeing weird creatures as of elemental essence.

'Elsie sees about a dozen fairies moving towards us in a crescent-shaped flight. As they draw near she remarks with ecstasy upon their perfect beauty of form; even while she does so, they become as ugly as sin, as if to give the lie to her words. They all leer at her and disappear. In this episode it may be that we contact a phase of the antagonism and dislike which so many of the fairy creatures feel for humans at this stage of evolution.

'Frances sees seven wee fairies quite near, weird little figures lying face downwards.'

'(In the Glen, August 18, 2 p.m.) Frances sees a fairy as big as herself, clothed in tights and with a garment scalloped round the hips; the garments are tight-fitting and flesh-coloured. The fairy has very large wings, which she opens above her head; then she raises her arms from her sides to above her head and waves them gracefully in the air. She has a very beautiful face, with an expression as if inviting Frances into fairyland. Her hair is apparently bobbed and the wings are transparent.'

Golden Fairy. 'One especially beautiful fairy has a body clothed in transparent shimmering golden light. She has tall wings, each of which is almost divided into upper and lower portions. The lower portion, which is smaller than the upper, appears to be elongated to a point, like the wings of some butterflies. She, too, is moving her arms and fluttering her wings. I can only describe her as a golden wonder. She smiles, and clearly sees us. She places her fingers on her lips. She remains in amongst the leaves and branches of the willow, watching us with smiling countenance. She is not objectively visible on the physical plane, only to astral sight. She points with her right hand, moving it in a circle round her feet, and I see a number of cherubs (winged faces), perhaps six or seven; these appear to be held in shape by some invisible will. She has cast a fairy spell over me, completely subjugating the mental principle. She leaves me staring wild-eyed in amongst the flowers and leaves.'

PART III

SOME LETTERS RECEIVED

Following the publication of the *Strand* articles and of Sir Arthur Conan Doyle's book *The Coming of the Fairies*, he and I both received a considerable number of letters from people who claimed to have seen fairies at some time in their lives or who were familiar with them continually. Some of the contacts made through this correspondence have already been mentioned in this book. Many of the letters were from well-known and reputable men and women and conveyed *bona fide* testimony, but one or two were deliberately fraudulent. All were examined carefully and sifted. I remember one photograph being sent in claiming to be a genuine picture of a little brownie at the foot of a tree. It was an outdoor single exposure shot and the natural character of the background was undoubted. When however our usual photographic analysis was made the figure of the brownie showed up at once as a clever artificial structure. When the author was challenged with this evidence he admitted the fact and excused the attempt by saying that he wished to prove that deception was possible by the use of built-up figures.

A selection is given here of some of the letters from persons where honesty and sincerity were unquestionable and who had from time to time seen the fairy people. Many of the statements made are corroborative of the evidence gleaned elsewhere.

From the Rev. Arnold J. Holmes: 'Being brought up in the Isle of Man one breathed the atmosphere of superstition (if you like to call it), the simple, beautiful faith of the Manx fisher folk, the childlike trust of the Manx girls, who to this day will not forget the bit of wood and coal put ready at the side of the fireplace in case the "little people" call and need a fire. A good husband is the ultimate reward, and neglect in this respect a bad husband or no husband at all. The startling phenomena occurred on my journey from Peel Town at night to St. Mark's (where I was Incumbent).

'After passing Sir Hall Caine's beautiful residence, Greeba Castle, my horse—a spirited one—suddenly stopped dead, and looking ahead I saw amid the obscure light and misty moonbeams what appeared to be a small army of indistinct figures—very small, clad in gossamer garments. They appeared to be perfectly happy, scampering and tripping along the road, having come from the direction of the beautiful sylvan glen of Greeba and St. Trinian's Roofless Church. The legend is that it has ever been the fairies' haunt, and when an attempt has been made on two occasions to put a roof on, the fairies have removed all the work during the night, and for a century no further attempts have been made. It has therefore been left to the "little people" who claim it as their own.

'I watched spellbound, my horse half mad with fear. The little happy army then turned in the direction of Witch's Hill, and mounted a mossy bank; one "little man" of larger stature than the rest, about fourteen inches high, stood at attention until all had passed him dancing, singing, with happy abandon, across the Valley fields towards St. John's Mount.'

From Mrs. Hardy. The wide distribution of the fairies may be judged by the following extremely interesting narrative from Mrs. Hardy, the wife of a settler in the Maori districts of New Zealand.

'After reading about what others have seen I am encouraged to tell you of an experience of my own which happened about five years ago. Will you please excuse my mentioning a few domestic details connected with the story? Our home is built on the top of a ridge. The ground was levelled for some distance to allow for sites for the house, buildings, lawns, etc. The ground on either side slopes steeply down, to an orchard on the left, and shrubbery and paddock on the right bounded by the main road. One evening when it was getting dusk I went into the yard to hang the tea-towels on the clothes-line. As I stepped off the verandah, I heard a sound of soft galloping coming from the direction of the orchard. I thought I must be mistaken, and that the sound came from the road, where the Maories often gallop their horses. I crossed the yard to get the pegs, and heard the galloping coming nearer. I walked to the clothes-line, and stood under it with my arms uplifted to peg the towel on the line, when I was aware of the galloping close behind me, and suddenly a little figure, riding a tiny pony, rode right under my uplifted arms. I looked round, to see that I was surrounded by eight or ten tiny figures on tiny ponies like dwarf Shetlands. The little figure who had come so close to me stood out quite clearly in the light that came from the window, but he had his back to it and I could not see his face. The faces of the others were quite brown, also the ponies were brown. If they wore clothes

42

they were close-fitting like a child's jersey suit. They were like tiny dwarfs, or children of about two years old. I was very startled, and called out, "Goodness, what is this?" I think I must have frightened them, for at the sound of my voice they all rode through the rose trellis across the drive, and down the shrubbery. I heard the soft galloping dying away into the distance, and listened until the sound was gone, then went into the house. My daughter, who has had several psychic experiences, said to me: "Mother, how white and startled you look! What have you seen? And who were you speaking to just now in the yard?" I said, "I have seen the fairies ride!" '

More New Zealand Fairies. New Zealand would appear to be quite a fairy centre, for I have another letter from a lady in those beautiful islands, which is hardly less interesting and definite than the one already quoted. She says:

'I have seen fairies in all parts of New Zealand, but especially in the fern-clad gullies of the North Island. Most of my unfoldment for mediumship was carried out in Auckland, and during that time I spent hours in my garden, and saw the fairies most often in the evening just before sunset. From observation I notice they usually live or else appear about the perennial plants. I saw brown fairies and green fairies, and they all had wings of a filmy appearance. I used to talk to them and ask them to make special pet plants and cuttings I put in the garden grow well, and I am sure they did, by the results I got. Since I came to Sydney I have also seen the green fairies. I tried an experiment last spring. I had some pheasant-eyed narcissus growing in the garden. I saw the garden fairies about them. I transplanted one of the bulbs to a pot when half-grown and took it with me when I went away for a short holiday. I asked the fairies to keep it growing. I watched it closely every evening—a green-clad fairy, sometimes one or two of them, would appear on the pot under the plant, and whatever they did to it during the night I do not know, but next morning it was very much bigger, and, although transplanted, etc., it flowered three weeks before those in the garden. I am now living in Rochdale, Sydney, with friends, both Australians and Spiritualists, and they also have seen the fairies from childhood up. I am sure animals see them. The fairies appear every evening in a little wild corner of the garden we leave for them, and our cat sits and watches them intently, but never attempts to spring at them, as he does at other moving objects. If you care to make use of the information contained in this letter, you are welcome to do so.'

From Australia. Another interesting letter, from Mrs. Roberts, of Australia, describes the intimate connection between these elemental forms of life and the flowers, and asserts that she has continually seen them tending the plants in her own garden.

A Leprechaun. Miss Hall, of Bristol, England, writes:

'I too, have seen fairies, but never until now have I dared to mention it for fear of ridicule. It was many years ago. I was a child of six or seven years, and

43

then, as now, passionately fond of all flowers, which always seem to me living creatures. I was seated in the middle of a road in some cornfields, playing with a group of poppies, and never shall I forget my utter astonishment at seeing a funny little man playing hide-and-seek amongst these flowers to amuse me, as I thought. He was quick as a dart. I watched him for quite a long time, then he disappeared. He seemed a merry little fellow, but I cannot ever remember his face. In colour he was sage-green, his limbs were round and had the appearance of geranium stalks. He did not seem to be clothed, and was about three inches high, and slender. I often looked for him again, but without success.'

Fairy Revel. Mr. J. Foot White, a well-known water diviner, writes:

'Some years ago I was one of a party invited to spend the afternoon on the lovely slopes of Oxeford Hill, in the County of Dorset. The absence of both trees and hedges in this locality enables one to see without obstruction for long distances. I was walking with my companion, who lives in the locality, some little distance from the main party, when to my astonishment I saw a number of what I thought to be very small children, about a score in number, and all dressed in little gaily-coloured short skirts, their legs being bare. Their hands were joined, and all held up, as they merrily danced round in a perfect circle. We stood watching them, when in an instant they all vanished from our sight. My companion told me they were fairies, and they often came to that particular part to hold their revels. It may be our presence disturbed them.'

Undines. Mrs. Ethel Enid Wilson, of Worthing, England, writes:

'I quite believe in fairies. Of course, they are really nature spirits. I have often seen them on fine sunny days playing in the sea, and riding on the waves, but no one I have ever been with at the time has been able to see them, excepting once my little nephews and nieces saw them too. They were like little dolls, quite small, with beautiful bright hair, and they were constantly moving and dancing about.'

Gnomes and Fairies. Mrs. Rose, of Southend-on-sea, told us in a chat on the subject:

'I think I have always seen fairies. I see them constantly here in the shrubbery by the sea. They congregate under the trees and float around about the trees, and gnomes come around to protect them. The gnomes are like little old men, with little green caps, and their clothes are generally neutral green. The fairies themselves are in light draperies. I have also seen them in the conservatory of my house, floating about among the flowers and plants. The fairies appear to be perpetually playing, excepting when they go to rest on the turf or in a tree, and I once saw a group of gnomes standing on each others' shoulders like gymnasts on the stage. They seem to be living as much as I am. It is not imagination. I have seen the gnomes arranging a sort of moss bed for the fairies, just like a mother-bird putting her chicks to bed. I don't hear any sounds from the gnomes or fairies, but they always look happy, as if they were having a real good time.'

PART IV
A SISTER STREAM OF EVOLVING LIFE

LATER EXPLORATIONS

The inquiry concerning the photographs taken in the Cottingley glen, a report of which is given so fully above, was followed during the next two or three years by a search for further information in order to discover the place such phenomena hold within the frame of their own appropriate order of life, and also to what extent and how intimately such an order might be related to our own. To this end I visited the Scottish Highlands, the New Forest in Hampshire, the Cumberland Lakes, Southern Ireland and many another likely haunt, to meet nature lovers, many of whom are clairvoyant, and to learn from them of their experiences.

Stories of fairies and their doings are abundant when one comes to look for them—but they were not my quest. I wanted to see and interview those who were acquainted at first-hand with the nature spirits and who were familiar in some measure with their habits and work and so could speak from direct personal experience. Although such evidence could not strictly be regarded as of a scientific quality, since trained clairvoyance is not yet a common faculty, it would be weighty if *bona fide* and corroborated, and could be tentatively accepted should the testimony have a sound practical and reasonable application. Two examples, among very many, of this kind of evidence will illustrate its character.

In Dundee a lecture on the Cottingley fairies had been arranged and the hall was crowded. At the conclusion questions and comment were invited and a gentleman in the front row rose at once and, speaking rather aggressively, said, 'The person I want to meet is one who can say, "I know such creatures exist, for I've seen them with my own eyes," but I have never come across that person.' Before I could reply, a woman stood up towards the back of the hall, a robust, pleasant-faced woman, and called out, 'Will the gentleman look this way?' Most of the audience did so, too, and then she said, 'Yes, I've seen them in plenty, these fairies, not just the same as the pictures tonight, but very like them. Anyhow, I know them well and have seen them with my own eyes, and there's any number round my way.' I spoke with her later and then visited Killiecrankie Pass, where she lived. Her interest and good faith were not to be doubted, and many of the details she gave me resembled closely facts that I had already collected.

In Dublin I had the good fortune to be introduced to George Russell, the Irish poet better known as A.E. During an afternoon we had an extremely interesting talk on nature spirits. A.E. told me, among other things, of his meeting with sylphs when on holiday near the west coast, an acquaintance which he had renewed year after year. Life-size pictures of the sylphs were painted on the walls of his sanctum, where we were seated. This experience of A.E.'s was the more remarkable by reason of the hostility that sylphs are reputed to feel towards humanity because of our careless pollution of their element, the air. But A.E.

45

had won through. The figures painted were about five feet high, not particularly handsome but very characteristic of the sylph when adopting human stature.

From the very considerable evidence obtained, on these lines and others more intimate, I have compiled some details of the ways of living and of the work of nature spirits. In many cases, when seeking information, I was interested to note that my share in making public the photographs taken in the Cottingley glen was a troublesome sort of introduction. Few fairy lovers look with favour on anything that gives publicity to the subject. Indeed, reproaches have been couched occasionally in no measured terms for what was regarded as an unwarranted intrusion and desecration on my part. Only after earnest assurances as to my own attitude could I get further and obtain those particulars which I have compared, checked and pieced together and can therefore set out here.

FUNCTION OF THE NATURE SPIRIT

Under the generic title of nature spirit are grouped several species, of which the gnome, brownie, fairy and undine are well-known varieties. In a classified system these would occupy almost the lowest place of a vast hierarchy. Mounting in graded steps from this level is a ladder of evolving life rising to the lofiest heights, the whole system composing a sister evolution on somewhat parallel lines to the animal and human kingdoms, but all using bodies of a subtler material than the physical. Many of the steps in this sister hierarchy are below the human rank and some are above, a few far above. The life of the nature spirit, nearly the lowest or outermost of all, is active in woodland, meadow and garden, in fact with vegetation everywhere, for its function is to furnish the vital connecting link between the stimulating energy of the sun and the raw material of the form-to-be. The growth of a plant from a seed, which we regard as the 'natural' result of its being placed in a warm and moist soil, could not happen unless nature's builders played their part. Just as music from an organ is not produced by merely bringing wind-pressure and a composer's score together, but needs also the vital link supplied by the organist, so must nature's craftsmen be present to weave and convert the constituents of the soil into the structure of a plant.

THE FAIRY BODY

The normal working body of the fairy sprites, used when they are engaged in assisting growth processes, is not of the human nor of any other definite form, and herein lies the explanation of much that has been puzzling concerning fairies and their kin. They have no clear-cut shape and their working bodies can be described only as clouds of colour, rather hazy, somewhat luminous, with a bright spark-like nucleus. They cannot, therefore, be defined in terms of clear-cut form, any more than one could so describe a tongue of flame. It is in this kind of body that they work, and inside, that is inter-penetrating, the plant structure. The cloud-like body seems to be of the nature of a magnetic field, for their constructive work in attending upon cell growth and assisting the circulation

46

of the sap resembles nothing so much as the movement of iron filings by a magnet, the magnetic influence being supplied by the currents of their own vital energies. Some nature spirits work above ground and some among the roots below. Others appear to specialise in colour and are responsible for the 'painting' of flowers, the needed brush being the streaming motion of their own cloud-like bodies. The growth of the plant depends also, of course, upon the presence or absence of essential food-stuffs and chemical constituents suitable to the plant's type. The presence or absence of any of these assist or limit the success of the performance much as the same condition applies to the human craftsman and artist. He can make do with poor stuff, but the best results come more easily with the best materials. So called 'sports' in plant forms and colourings are sometimes merely the result of faulty work though there is evidence that occasionally they are due to a strong desire-form mentally created by a human being.

Yet there is little trace of any intelligent direction or selection on the part of these builders, for their work appears to be wholly instinctual. The level of their consciousness seems to be about that of young animals, birds and insects, and their labours are directed by some influence which resembles closely the same instinctual prompting that marks the surprisingly purposive actions of ants and bees.

THE HUMAN FORM

Although the nature spirit must be regarded as irresponsible, living seemingly a gladsome, joyous and untroubled life, with an eager enjoyment of its work, it occasionally leaves that work and steps out of the plant, as it were, and instantly changes its shape into that of a diminutive human being, not necessarily then visible to ordinary sight but quite near to the range of visibility. Assumed in a flash, it may disappear as quickly. While the human shape is retained it seems evident that, by reason perhaps of its concrete and definite form, it gives an added sense of enjoyment. Within the form there is, however, no organisation that is perceptible; the content of the new-shaped body is merely that of the normal cloud-body condensed. When the human form is adopted the nature spirit usually begins to skip and dance and exhibit a gay abandon suggestive of its keen delight in the experience. If disturbed or alarmed, the change back to the diffused magnetic cloud is as sudden as its emergence. Why the human shape is nearly always assumed is not clear; it may be that human thinking, by the individual or in the mass, is the stimulus and cause—but this is conjecture. Sometimes other shapes are adopted, such as insect and animal forms, the tendency being to copy a model in the vicinity, not to invent, and the human form seems to be the most attractive. One point is certain: the nature spirit form, whether in its normal cloud-like working body or when in the human shape, is objective, and thus dimensional.

FAIRY WINGS

Anatomically one would not expect to find wings, frequently seen as a feature

47

of the fairy body, in conjunction with arms. But there is no articulation, no venation, and the wings are not used for flying. Their undoubted appearance may be due, again, to human thought. Humanity's conception of an angelic host has usually included both wings and arms. Sometimes, though, from the head and shoulders of the nature spirit, instead of well-formed wings, there is a streaming misty cloud, coloured, very suggestive of the elaborate head-dresses of the Red Indian. More than one observer spoke of the resemblance as being so close that 'probably the Red Indians copied what someone or other had seen.'

FOOD, BIRTH AND DEATH

Nourishment in abundance, and apparently ample for sustenance, is absorbed directly into the cloud body by a rhythmic pulsing movement that is continuous. Breathing is the nearest analogy.

There is no birth, nor death, as we understand the terms, but simply an emergence from and a return to a subtler state of existence. The process is gradual. In this subtler state there appears to be a larger unit from which the cloud-like body of a typical nature spirit is budded off in a fashion which resembles the fission and budding-off of our familiar animalcules—with the addition that, towards the end of the cycle of emergence, there is a fusion or reassembly back into the larger unit.

SPEECH

Amongst the lesser builders, whose province is earth and water, there appears to be nothing in the way of language. Communication between a human being and the nature spirit is possible only by sound and gesture, much as the same can be employed for calling domestic animals. Indeed, the human relationship to many of them seems to be about on a par with that between humans and puppies or kittens: perhaps it can be called a tone language, but that is all.

THE PLANT KINGDOM GENERALLY AND NATURE SPIRITS

There is, of course, a life of the vegetable kingdom apart from that of the nature spirit builders. Plant life, slowly differentiating and thus specialising itself through the many forms of the kingdom, is, however, very little more than just conscious—that is, vaguely aware of existence in a physical form. An ancient saying bears on this and is worth repeating: 'God sleeps in the mineral, dreams in the plant, stirs in the animal and awakes in man.' Dreaming, slumbering, well describes the life of the plant kingdom itself. The nature spirit craftsmen, building and tending the forms which this dreaming life uses, are, on the other hand, very busily awake. The relation of the life of the plant itself to the nature spirits may be well illustrated by the relation between passengers on a ship and the officers and crew who navigate it. The crew are the workers, the passengers are merely being carried. Similarly, the life of the vegetable kingdom is little more active than that of a passenger being carried from port to port. One may presume that

48

the plant life, on its journey from the mineral kingdom to the animal, is not only carried but, to some extent, is stimulated, fostered and advanced through the activities of the nature spirit builders. Humanity, also, takes a hand in this education of the plant kingdom. The assistance given by man, both to the life of the vegetable kingdom and to the nature spirits, is seen in the vast variety of cultivated flowers, shrubs, trees and fruits, achieved by human skill in selection and training. Although man's co-operation with nature's hidden workers may at present be prompted largely by our own desires, the partnership, when appreciated as such, will certainly yield many more delightful developments in the evolution of new flowers and fruits.

HUMAN AND DEVA*

From the above it will be seen how very many contacts are being made between human beings and the devic hosts in agriculture and horticulture. This relationship may become intimate indeed when one is intent on developing some new speciality in flower or fruit growing, for then, quite unconsciously perhaps, a cordial partnership is at work, however little it be realised by either side. Some people, however, are intuitively aware of this and vividly so. Man provides the will and the wishful-desire elements in such work and the devic ranks supply the craftsmen. It is a fair division and a rather strict one for neither can encroach much on the other's province—and it is worth noting how very much man has contributed to the partnership in the way of increasing and greatly improving varieties and quality. As 'nature' gets so much commendation an anecdote may be permitted here. An allotment was being worked by an elderly man and the vegetables were coming along well when the vicar, passing by, stopped and had a word. 'Ah! William,' said he, 'isn't it wonderful what God and man can do together?' William was not impressed; and replied 'Dunno about that, parson. You should h'seen the place when God had it alone!' The partnership between man and the devic hosts is really a fair one, for both sides are gaining experiences. By trial and error mankind is learning a good deal about what is needed to ensure the best conditions as to soil-composition, moisture and warmth—a very important contribution, though the resulting growth of seed, slip-cutting, graft or bud is entirely the work of the devic partner.

One of the many questions on which I have endeavoured to get some light has been whether a human being can exercise much influence over the nature spirit craftsmen. We have all found, I expect, that some people are more successful with flowers than are others. Most of us know a 'Gladys, she just shoves 'em in and golly how they grow,' as the poet put it. Some friendly people will keep flowers in bowls and vases looking fresh and happy for a week and more while, with others, the flowers fade away in half the time. Why?

An answer on the right lines is to be found, I believe, in the human being's

* Deva: literally 'shining one'; western equivalent, angel.

49

emotional nature. During my fairy quest I was aware again and again of a subtle solicitude and kindliness on the part of the nature spirit lover for everything in the way of flowers and shrubs and trees. This deep-seated attitude of mind and heart seems to be the most telling and persuasive influence that a man or woman can bring to bear, though it may in many cases be used quite unconsciously. To this the nature spirit, and the deva world generally, respond. It is true, however, that such an attitude of thought and feeling cannot be improvised and mentally distributed just when one thinks of it—the roots of that power are deeper than that, being nurtured in the warmth of a heart-felt emotional sincerity. Human thinking, human passion, human anger, human kindliness and affection, all have far-reaching effects, for the devic hosts in their subtle ethereal bodies live in an atmosphere where thought and feeling are very real forces. Though a clear understanding between human and deva may be a long way off yet, it is worth knowing that our feelings and thoughts, though maybe unconsciously expressed, influence the devic hosts about us and lead us to reactions that can be helpful or obstructive—to us.

CONSCIOUSNESS: VERTICAL AND HORIZONTAL

Myth, legend and folk-lore, and the scriptures of most religions, teem with allusions to another order of living beings, all of whom use bodies of a subtler texture than visible to the ordinary physical sight. Many are the names given to these beings—archangels and angels, maha-devas and devas, genii, demons; and the more familiar salamanders, sylphs, undines and gnomes associated respectively with the elements of fire, air, water and earth. Also, under the generic term nature spirits, as already mentioned, there is a vast array connected with the germination of seeds, the growth and upkeep of trees, shrubs and flowers, indeed with the whole vegetable kingdom, concerning which descriptive testimony has already been given.

The word 'deva', meaning simply 'shining one', is non-committal and appropriate, hence I propose calling this vast sister-stream of evolving life the devic evolution. Their ranks, apparently, constitute a hierarchy linking the loftiest regions to those that, materially, are most remote from pure spirit. A general principle, which emerges from a study of the evidence available, can be advanced with some confidence as being true. This is that the devic evolution possesses what I must call vertical consciousness; which means that their numerous ranks function as a unitary whole from the highest levels to the physical, without any break. On the other hand and in contrast, humanity must be said to possess horizontal consciousness, for man normally has no conscious link with a higher or lower rank than his own. For example, the animal kingdom is distinct and separate in consciousness from ourselves and, though the gulf is not impassable, it is wide. A similar gulf separates man from any ranks above his own; though again, this can be bridged by deliberate effort. Human consciousness, thus

50

horizontally developed as compared with the devic, nevertheless has latent within it the ability to make contact with the whole gamut of the devic hosts, by virtue of the composite constitution with which man is endowed.

Although the consciousness of humanity as a whole works chiefly on the horizontal level, as described above, nevertheless in the case of a single human individual we have an excellent illustration of 'vertical' consciousness. Connecting a man's brain with his hands is a nerve chain composed of many links. The hands of a skilled craftsman will respond quickly to the orders sent from the brain although, on their way, these traverse a lengthy ladder of nerve ganglia and muscular tissue. Suppose now that only these busy hands of the craftsman were seen; nothing, say, above the wrist. Then the orderly and constructive movements of the fingers would be called instinctive; that is, the hand and fingers would be regarded as inspired from a source within themselves. In the man a connecting chain of clearly defined links can be traced from the brain to the extremities of the body and the means of communication may be called that of a wired system. In the devic order, each rank of the hierarchy is composed of specialists concerned with particular and specific tasks divided between rank and rank. The system of communication is without any visible connecting mechanism, for it works on a wireless model, a radio system. From the loftiest heights, in the unseen where mental archetypes exist, right through to the densest regions of physical material, the communicating system of this band of ordered workers appears to extend. The elaborate detail of the concrete and specialised forms of the kingdoms of nature owe their construction to the active 'fingers' at the lower extremity of the devic consciousness; these fingers being represented by the nature spirits in their vast totality. All are prompted and guided by precise impulses received through the devic system of communication. Failing a rational explanation of the amazing skill displayed in the building of nature's forms, we say that it is due to instinct. If we had 'sight' we should perceive that from the devic mathematical genii, just beneath the level of the archetypal world, down to the physical level, the impulses directing growth travel, step by step, very similarly to impulses travelling from, say, a musician's brain to his fingers. The consciousness of the devas is widely spaced and loosely knit, for each rank, as said, has a specialised task only: the musician's system of communications is closely packed within the limits of a single personality. Very wonderfully, in the human constitution there are elements corresponding to every rank of the devic hosts, so the possibility exists, though latent at present, of inter-communication between human and deva.

AN EXAMPLE OF VERTICAL CONSCIOUSNESS IN THE DEVIC RANKS

The statement of the existence of the principle, called vertical consciousness, is not based on mere conjecture and inference but is grounded on direct observation, up to certain level. This line of observation began, in the first place,

51

with a group of tall flowers, michaelmas daisies, which were nearing maturity. The nature spirits, working within the plants in their small, spherical, pulsing bodies, each a field of magnetic activity, were seen to be connected, each one, as it were by a thread of light, to a worker in the next higher rank, So, at least, the relationship appeared, for many such magnetic 'threads' were collected together and held in one centre or knot—as the human hand would hold the reins of a team of horses. From the workers of the higher rank, again, lines or threads of light rose to be held joined at a yet higher level. Many similar observations and instances support the view that the physical workers, the nature spirits of the plant kingdom in the case mentioned, are subtly linked to the next rank above in the devic order—with the reasonable inference that the linkage continues to the highest. This continuum of consciousness in the devic order is reminiscent of the age-old story of the prodigal son and the elder brother. If the prodigal represents humanity, as is usually assumed, then the elder brother appropriately represents the devic order. He, the elder, has never left his father's house, never ceased to follow the paternal instructions—'Son, thou art ever with me and all that I have is thine' (Luke xv). The resentment against human beings felt by certain ranks of the devas, the sylphs for instance, is true to the story also.

INSTINCT

The work of the nature spirits in the building and care of the forms, the physical bodies, of the mineral, plant, animal and human kingdoms (for they have their task in each) is obscured by the common use of the very inadequate term instinct. In the light of the above descriptions a reasonable explanation is given of instinct's very many puzzling problems. From the observations recorded it would seem certain that in the devic hierarchy is to be found the responsible source of all so-called instinctual behaviour. In the directive instruction given by the devic hosts lies the secret of the wonderful ability of newly born insects, birds, and animals, to look after themselves in varying degrees, as also the amazing but apparently untutored skill of the parents so often displayed in providing the necessary safe refuges and nests for their progeny. Instinct, in all its baffling varieties of expression, is at least understandable if we accept it as a manifestation of the hidden existence of the devic order, our sister stream of evolving life.

DEVIC COMPETITION

A further vista is opened when we consider the competitive skill displayed in camouflage and mimicry, adopted by many plants and animals in self-defence. But these antagonisms and rivalries among the middle ranks of the devas, which seem to be indicated by strife among their charges, may be and probably is, merely due to the urgent interior drive they feel to help those under their special care. Obviously the forms produced in such profusion in the physical kingdoms of nature are the result of endless experiments, of much trial and error, quickened by competition and the deletion of the unfit. In the devic order are to be found the architects, builders and craftsmen of Mother Nature, all linked in an intimate co-relationship. A prodigality of form is perfectly natural to them; the many that are discarded, or destroyed, are not wasted any more than are the try-out sketches of an artist which pave the way to a successful picture.

HUMAN AND DEVA ARE COMPLEMENTARY

These two streams of evolutionary life, human and devic, though in many aspects opposites, are vitally and very wonderfully complementary. With horizontal and vertical types of consciousness respectively they may well be regarded as making up the warp and weft of the garment of manifestation. The devic hosts are imbued with a direct awareness of divine law; they 'live but to do the will of the Father' as an old phrase has it, but the 'awareness' of each rank is strictly limited to that part of nature's scheme upon which for the time being any group is engaged. Man, on the other hand, has a sense of individual responsibility, can critically analyse, can exercise discretion and choice, and has extensive 'horizontal' control over a very wide range of nature's field. The problem to face and the task to achieve is for humanity and the devas to know each other better. At the present time we weave back and forth very unaware of the work of the devas, and the devic life on its side is often thwarted and even repelled by man's ignorant and crude intrusions.

There are fortunately signs of change—as in the recent developments towards less extravagantly artificial systems of fostering plant and animal growth and production, and in the recognition and respect for natural methods and natural rhythms as yielding in the long run the best results. In agriculture and allied sciences all this is increasingly in evidence. In medical practice also a revolutionary change is likely to accompany the recognition of living through unseen craftsmen as being the immediate creative form-builders.

That which we call natural law is indeed made effective through a vast hierarchy of intelligent beings and, as we yield to them an intelligent co-operation, the dawn of a new and loftier cycle in our world's evolution must begin.